BY SILVIA M

Romantic

TWIN FLAMES

A NEWBIES GUIDE

Silvia Moon

Twin Flame Romance

For all twin flames going through your
Awakening phases

Meeting a Romantic Twin Flame

Is it common for twin flames to end up together in real life? If so, how does this dynamic work? If not, what is the purpose of twin flames coming into our lives?

I believe that it is true and common for twin flames to end up together. It is your typical "Cinderella Story" — meeting a twin flame feels that way too. It's like a fairytale feeling. Somehow you talk to yourself wondering; "This is how it feels to find true love?" "I can't believe it's me feeling this way!" "Is this real or is my mind playing tricks?" "Am I dreaming?"

If you haven't awakened yet and realized how special a twin flame is, the questions you have in your mind overwhelm you and you feel unworthy and undeserving of pure potent unconditional love. Depending on how much trauma and fears you have, you deny your twin flame altogether because you are better off feeling trapped within yourself than breaking free to face whatever is scaring you.

Romantic Twin Flame Fun Facts

Even though you feel overwhelmed by your twin flame connection, you feel pleased and grateful for knowing the feeling of unconditional love. It is a blessing to know pure love right from the Source. You feel complete — you feel whole. You are happy to find an equal match. Another you in another person.

After you find know a twin flame exists, you never forget their eyes and how they make you feel. You miss yourself whenever you are in physical separation. You have your twin flame's memories playing in the background of your life keeping them alive in every moment of your life. You cannot help but look back on how happy you felt in your twin flame's presence. Sometimes you deliberately think of a twin flame because it feels good to miss and remember them. Even though you are going through tough life situations, thinking of a twin flame is your form of escape. This is also the reason why telepathic communication is intensified during separation. You pull each other into the connection by remembering a twin flame.

Twin flames can end up together in real life because even though your separation phase drags on you are both willing to work on it. Suppose you both desire to reunite shortly. It means that even though the going gets tough, you stick together with understanding and unconditional love even though you don't share the same physical space. You keep your communication channels open. You also both understand that Long-distance relationships are tough.

The main purpose of twin flames coming into our lives is to help us to Awaken to ourselves, to love, life, and our life purpose. These events happen through a series of Spiritual Awakening and Growth. Through Soul lessons and alchemical changes that happen psychologically, physically, spiritually, and emotionally.

Physical Separation Blessings

Can being separated from your twin flame strengthen your connection?

From a running twin flame perspective, physical separation indeed strengthens the connection. The best word is; Intensity. The connection is intensified indeed. I believe this is so because it is a form of compromise. When you have no choice but to accept how you feel and allow yourself to tap into the energetic connection. Whenever you engage your spiritual and energetic connection, it changes your separation dynamic. You first realize that separation is just an illusion because you feel him or her whenever you are aligned energetically. Whenever you learn to embrace your telepathic connection, you learn that you feel a twin whether they are with you. Telepathy is one of the most distinct ways to prove that you are going through an authentic twin flame experience. Sometimes your doubts seem to convince you that you are delusional. That you are being obsessive and making it all up. You still feel the connection nonetheless. You cannot control the connection. Your twin flame's essence invades your space. You hear mental conversations initiated by your twin flame.

Finding a married Twin Flame

Can a person who is married still feel a connection with their twin flame?

A twin flame who is married can feel the connection as much as a twin flame who is single. It is a total nightmare for both twin flames because you are not free to express how you feel for each other. When it comes to a twin flame, you cannot stay away from each other because you feel a magnetic attraction — a Soul pulling that cannot be controlled by you or your twin flame. It is very excruciating watching your twin flame happy in a relationship with someone else because you always wish it was you. Just because someone is your twin flame, it does not mean that they can't be happy with someone else. Sometimes all you can do is keep moving on with your life and hope to have a chance whenever your twin flame is available. For a married twin flame, you still go through all the stages of awakening like the night of the soul. Twin Flames deserve to be in a harmonious Union Forever because separation hurts — life without hope to be with a twin flame is miserable and lonely.

Divine Feminine Energy

Why does a twin flame divine feminine run?

I was a runner too. Here are reasons for running:

Insecurities — a twin flame connection disarms you, leaving you vulnerable and disoriented. If you have abandonment issues, you automatically feel unworthy and undeserving of an authentic connection. You keep wondering to yourself; "Is this real?" You think the Universe is playing tricks on you.

The twin flame bond is so unreal — it's that feeling that drives you crazy because you assume you are being obsessive or delusional. You can also easily explain it to anyone who hasn't been through the experience. It is also very antagonistic because you don't know what to do if you have never heard of the twin flame phenomenon. It is worse if you are married. That is another whole issue trying to navigate your situation.

It is more complicated if you have people relying on you like family, kids, and extended family because you still go through the spiritual awakening process. You struggle with balancing your energy — you go through mood swings. You feel irritable and frustrated by the energetic turbulence. The twin flame process is an energetic draining process. You cannot help yourself but feel restless and helpless, especially through the night of the soul. The twin flame journey is a battle within self indeed.

Reunion Aspirations

What does a miraculous reunion look like on a twin flame journey?

There is a huge difference between a reunion and a union. Phew! Union is when you merge your inner self. That is why we struggle during the night of the soul. Just to find ourselves. Our authenticity.

A reunion with a twin flame eventually happens whether you like it or not. Some twin flames deny it all the time — just when the going gets rough, all the disbelief, doubts, and insecurities kick in. We must all say that finding your twin flame disarms you and makes you feel vulnerable. The truth is the twin flame experience is as disorienting as it gets.

Signs of Healing

Emotional uncontrolled outbursts — whenever he or she has mood swings, know that your twin flame is struggling with some form of emotional pain. They feel some sensitivity that you feel like you are walking on eggshells around them. If your twin flame is also acting insecure and unhinged because they are still struggling with themselves. Abandonment issues can trigger your self-esteem issues. Anger issues — whenever you are going through the night of the soul, you feel unhinged, erratic, and easily annoyed. You feel like you are going through an emotional rollercoaster indeed.

Dealing with Negative Energy

What factors contribute to the level of negativity between Twin Flames?

Whenever you are asked to confront parts of yourself that you hid from previously, you go through a series of inner turmoil and emotional turbulence in which your fears are triggered. Your insecurities are triggered. Your abandonment issues come to the surface. You feel your wounding exposed as you explore the depths of your soul to confront your pain. It could be that you had been repressing grief, pain, anger, fear, guilt, and shame. Whatever you are hiding from within yourself comes to light when you experience the night of the soul.

This is the most challenging of all phases because you have nowhere to run but to confront your darkness — your inner pain. The most challenging phase of all is traveling back within yourself to hug your suffering inner child. This is a self-disintegration process. A self-rediscovery process. You must learn to tame the ego and break free from whatever pain was blocking you from feeling yourself at the core to be in touch with your authenticity. Your inner child is the beginning of everything — healing, happiness, self-discovery, and unending inner harmony.

To answer your question, whenever a twin flame is struggling with its healing process. They could be avoiding facing their fears and inner pain because of deep-seated trauma. They could have triggered abandonment issues that he or she is feeling powerless to face the darkness they hid away. from for so long hoping never to open the Pandora box again. Sometimes it is the feeling of guilt and shame of confronting deep-seated pain. You feel irritable, and angry because you are opening up all your repressed pain. You are constantly shedding layers of negative energy. It is an energy cleansing and purification process.

If a twin flame is not ready to confront these issues, there will be different levels of negativity including running away from each other and pretending everything will be okay. Unfortunately, you can run all you want. You will eventually go through it all. Your innermost unconfronted pain will bring you to your knees. Your ego will be tamed. Your heart will break open to embrace unconditional love. Light will enter your wounds. You will heal. You will find your authentic self.

Is Ghosting You Forever?

Even though TF runners do everything possible to block the chaser's efforts and deny the connection on every level, do they still read messages, emails, etc.?

Twin Flame runners are always the enigma. Their behaviors are quite confusing and it is energetically draining trying to solve the puzzle of a running twin flame. Whenever you chase a twin flame, they read your messages even though they keep saying nothing back. It is frustrating when all you need is a runner to say something but nothing yet your delivery notifications show your messages received and sometimes read instantly.

A twin flame goes through so much torture and confusion because their pain and fear are within themselves. He or she is struggling with confronting themselves. A twin flame can stalk you in the most stealthy way possible. It is because it is challenging not to think of a twin flame. On top of that, the connection eats you from within. You go through all the phases of spiritual awakening. You cannot stop yourself from the energetic pulling. All twin flame runners must admit that it is always lovely to hear from a twin flame even though it is overwhelming. Confusing and emotionally chaotic. Whenever you receive a message from a twin flame, you feel butterflies in your stomach. Your stomach churns whenever you see a twin flame ringing you on the phone.

Channeling each other's energy

Why do I feel a twin flame's energy in submission?

You always feel your twin flame's energy at every step of your twin flame journey. Whenever you find healing and surrender — you feel your shared energy more strongly wherever you are even though you have been physically separated for the longest time. Whenever you are separated from a twin flame and feel your connection more intensely, it is a sign that separation is an illusion — you always feel connected to each other whether you are in denial or not.

Surrendering frees you from every stress — whenever you learn to draw back your energy and focus on healing, you feel your connection more strongly because your channel feels clearer. Your telepathic channel is more open and the more you feel connected, the more you relax and trust that everything will eventually be okay no matter how far separation from each other takes you.

Runner's Perspective

How does a twin flame runner view their journey and the time spent apart from their twin flame?

If the running twin flame has not yet realized what is happening between you and them, chasing only amplifies their running behaviors. It gets to a point when a twin flame runs and blocks you because you keep triggering him or her to remember themselves. They are afraid of awakening themselves. Sometimes it is the fear of feeling overwhelmed by the intense feelings that the connection brings. Sometimes just feeling unconditional love for your twin flame disarms you. You feel vulnerable that running away is your temporary fix. It is never easy whenever your partner keeps chasing you even though you ghost them. You feel more frustrated.

Blocking thoughts of a twin flame

Is it possible to mentally block thoughts about our twin flames?

You can block thoughts of your twin flame temporarily but somehow you are triggered to think of them in the back of your mind even though you are not actively missing him or her. The worst experience when you block thoughts of a twin flame is when you feel disconnected within. You feel as if you are trying to block certain parts of yourself just because you are actively trying to not think of a twin flame. Whenever you resist the flow of the connection within. When you also try your best to block telepathic communication because, at the end of the day, telepathy can get annoying whenever you don't want to miss your beloved.

For me, I always feel energetically blocked. I don't do anything creative. I also feel helpless and restless whenever I block myself from feeling the connection. I never feel any form of inner peace only because of blocking the twin flame connection.

Letting go

Is it necessary to love your twin flame? If not, why is it difficult to let go of them?

It is not necessary to love your twin flame because it is a natural connection. Everything comes naturally to you while you are with a twin flame. Whenever you meet a twin flame, you are in awe! you keep wondering how it is possible to know someone who is another version of you. You feel so close to them that you want to talk to him or her constantly. Your attraction is not sexual because it is Sacred and something you both acknowledge that was meant to happen. You know in your Soul that your encounter is not a coincidence but something aligned at the start. Divinity and the Universe connived to bring you two together. Sometimes our minds cannot comprehend what the Twin Flame journey is all about.

The main reason why it feels impossible to let a twin flame go is because of soul intimacy. Your soul connection makes it impossible to forget each other. You feel your twin flame inside you. Your essence keeps merging with yours. You see their face in your mind. You dream of a twin flame. Whether a twin flame is with you or not, you feel haunted by the spiritual and energetic connection.

Dealing with a running twin flame

Is it normal for the twin flame runner to deny the twin flame phenomenon?

It is very normal to deny the connection. The running twin flame is never comfortable with how they feel. They are sometimes unaware of the twin flame phenomenon. Running is out of all fears and deep-seated pain. You never know what sets them off exactly. Even though you think your life is going well, a twin flame can abruptly block you mainly because you are triggering them to feel all sorts of uncomfortable feelings. Sometimes a twin flame runs mainly because they realise that you love them unconditionally and the vulnerability scares them off if he or she never felt loved before meeting you. A running twin flame is always perplexed by the situation because even though you run and hide, the connection is embedded within. You feel energetically intertwined.

Feeling happy during separation

Is it okay that I no longer have any desire for union with my Twin? I want him to know he is loved and I do not want him to fear me or avoid me. But I have no desire to create a life with him any longer. Has anyone else experienced this?

It is okay and normal to no longer have desires for a physically romantic relationship with a twin flame. You have to also know that having a relationship with a twin flame is not the epitome of the twin flame journey. The time comes when you are happy on your own without needing validation from him or her. When you reach the healing phase your inner peace is all that matters to you. You also realize that whether a twin flame desires a relationship with you or not, life has to keep moving forward. The essence of the twin flame journey is acting on your awareness and awakening. You go through spiritual healing and growth. You ascend and transcend the needs of the ego. You are no longer controlled by lustful desires. You transform into an authentic being.

Is it possible for a twin flame relationship to end without any contact?

Well, you cannot tell how God/universe works. Just the same way you met your twin flame — you were surprised to know that someone else like you walks the earth somewhere. More so, the encounter was also unplanned. You didn't know about twin flames until you met him or her.

The other important thing to remember is that a twin flame connection is very different from having a relationship with your twin flame. Also, not all twin flame connections culminate into romantic relationships. A romantic twin flame encounter is a different dynamic altogether because all you crave and desire is to be in a harmonious Union one day. You may desire to get married and create a beautiful family life together.

Even though the separation phase drags on, a romantic twin flame will crave for you as much as you crave for them because you both know that finding each other was one of the luckiest days of your life. You feel like you have won a lottery of love — you also feel grateful to be one of the lucky few people in this world who know the meaning of unconditional love.

People fall in love but Twin Flame is your perfect fairytale story — it is how you are with a twin flame that boggles your mind. You don't need words to explain to a twin flame how you feel and neither do they have to say anything. The connection is unspoken and indescribable.

To answer your question, if it is an authentic twin flame connection, your Spiritual connection will always remind you where you are. You think of each other and miss your twin flame from within. There is always a part of you that is lonely — an empty void that only a twin flame's presence can feel. That alone and the energetic pulling are enough to bring you back to each other for a reconciliation. Keep trusting the process of your twin flame journey. Believe in the connection.

Reunion Signs

What are the signs of a twin flame reunion? Can a twin flame reunion occur without any contact?

Doesn't your initial Twin Flame encounter feel like a reunion in itself? It felt as if you had lived a past life — you keep wondering how you know him or her even though it is your first time meeting them. You feel an uncanny familiarity with a stranger. Everything you talk about is not new to your soul. Your conversations sound as if you are catching up from where you left off. Meeting a twin flame is one of the most surprising strangest things in the world. It is also an earthmoving experience looking into your twin flame's eyes. You can see their Soul. It is a magical thing to acknowledge each other. If you are physically separated from a twin flame without contact, do not worry or stress about it. Firstly, it is not the end of the world and your connection. It takes a while to break free from the typical normal templates of love to fully acknowledge the spiritual nature of your connection. Once you understand that separation from a twin flame is an illusion, then you learn to focus on embracing your healing journey while you prepare yourself for the reunion.

The reunion with a twin flame is an event. The question to ask is; "How ready are you to reunite with your twin flame?"

Is it common for twin flames to reunite permanently?

ometimes we blame our twin flames for causing the prolonged separation phases yet we are the cause. It is easier to cast the blame on your twin flame because of projection. If you know who your twin flame is and you both acknowledge the connection, there is no way you will stay apart. Somehow you won't let each other go even though you have so many obstacles to surmount. You dream of each other and your deepest desire is to one day have a stable harmonious relationship. A permanent twin flame reunion is possible if you both work hard at it. Just like any other normal relationship, your physical participation is required even though you share a sacred connection.

Remember to do the following:

Keep communication channels open

Share your experiences, especially your healing journeys

Become friends instead of enemies of foes

Be more empathetic and understanding of each other

You only have one twin flame — embrace it instead of resisting it.
Work on your issues now to avoid them being future blockages

Runner Flipping and Flopping

When the DM twin flame runner awakens to the connection, why doesn't he come back to the chaser and keep running?

It could be that the chaser is still stuck in a karmic relationship — separation is not about the running twin flame. It could be that the chasing twin flame is the one who has more karmic debts to clear. Sometimes you chase a twin flame because you have not yet accepted to confront your issues hoping that your twin flame partner will save you from yourself.

Healing is a gradual process that takes time — a twin flame awakening only amplifies your inner pain and core wounding to be exposed. You go through different phases of healing and this can take as long as it does. Meanwhile, your twin flame's life has to move forward. They also go through different healing processes and spiritual awakenings.

It is not about having a physical relationship — The essence of the twin flame journey is not your physical relationship. Your spiritual growth and healing are the epitome of the journey.

The running twin flame is always present in your life even though you are unaware of it. They are always keeping tabs on you because they miss you as much as you miss them.

The Eternal Bond

Is it possible for a twin flame to stay with their partner until the end of their life?

Yes. A romantic twin flame pair can find each other and stay together harmoniously without any rifts and frustrations that most twin flames go through when there is no more healing. Some twin flames find each other when they have both gone through some healing phases that their encounter only heals them further and binds them into a Spiritual and physical Union. Those are the couples that you when watching them as they are together heal you. Being in their space and sharing energy with a twin flame pair is blissful. Twin flame love is potent, pure, and effortless.

Whenever you meet your divine partner, you automatically know they are the one. You know you have found what your soul was searching for even though you previously had no idea who it was. You feel content and peaceful within. You know that everything will eventually be alright. Every painful experience you have ever gone through seems to fade away and all that is left is healing and unconditional love.

A twin flame connection frees you from any fears, insecurities, guilt, shame, and worthlessness. For the first time in your life, you feel important because you are inspired to pursue meaningful life prospects. You start caring about the human collective — you know you can't save the world but you desire to create meaningful changes in your little corner of the world. The beauty of it all is; that the twin flame connection inspires you to become your best highest self through spiritual, psychological, emotional, and physical transformations.

Who wouldn't take the chance to be with a twin flame forever?

Twin Flame Vs Soulmates

How can one determine if they have a twin flame or multiple soulmates? How can we differentiate between these connections?

Well, one truth I know is that a twin flame connection is very unique from soulmate connections. Firstly, with a soulmate, you feel ready and free to let them go when the time comes for a separation. You easily accept defeat and even though it takes you a long to pick yourself up, you figure it out soon or late. You surrender right away to the heartbreak and you accept your life situation. The other thing about soulmate connections is that there is that invisible feeling of tit for tat that makes the relationship feel more or less conditional, unlike the twin flame dynamic. You feel as if you have some form of control to some extent. You can also compromise with how much love and care to give.

When it comes to twin flames, the dynamic is frustrating because even though you wish to separate from a twin flame and forget them, your soul is stronger than your wishes. You naturally feel magnetically connected to this person that inner resistance to what is happening can only bring you more pain and suffering. The other thing is that twin flame love is so profound that you feel unworthy of it if you have hidden inner pain or you are running away from your fears and insecurities. You must face all your demons and heal your core wounding to feel deserving of unconditional love. That is one of the reasons why some twin flames who are not ready to face themselves come up with all sorts of excuses to deny the connection.

When you find a twin flame, you go all in with your cards. It's all or nothing. You don't think about being hurt or betrayed since you have a connection that transcends the barriers of loving someone. Finding yourself in another person is a special thing. When you know, you know.

Runner Refuses to return

What are some possible reasons for a twin flame runner to not want to return?

There are so many distractions out there. If a twin flame is running, he or she can jump into a new karmic relationship thinking they will forget what just happened to them. Other twin flames who were previously married tend to run back to fix their marriages and relationships realizing that the changes happening in your life after the encounter will destabilize your life as you know it.

Not every twin flame is willing to open their heart to go through the overwhelming healing journey and the intense spiritual awakening processes. More so, if a twin flame finds you in a happy stable relationship, it is not easy to separate your family. Maybe your finances are merged with your husband or partner. There are so many variable factors that can make a twin flame run and also not want to return.

I always advise fellow twin flame to be careful with what kind of relationships you enter during the separation phase. You might think that your twin flame will realize you over them to attract them back but it only pushes her or him further away because you seem happy with someone new. Even though the twin flame experience is a spiritual journey, we are still human and going through our 3D lives. Try not to hurt your twin flame with your actions just because you are provoking them. Focus on yourself and keep learning your Spiritual Growth Lessons.

Reaching out then ghosting

Why does a runner twin flame reach out and then ghost?

The fear of losing you — a twin flame who is running will suddenly reach out to you just because they want to make sure that you are still there. To make sure you are still caring and thinking of him or her. Sometimes a twin flame will run just to see if you will chase them out of fears of losing you and insecurities of not feeling worthy of being loved. Therefore, a runner will check in to have a measure of the temperature because, at the end of the day, they feel the connection as much as you do.

They can't stop thinking of you and wondering how you are faring.

The need to be triggered to heal further — Have you also noticed that a twin flame will pop back into your life because they are still healing? The moment you say or do something that triggers them, they will block you and ghost you for another round.

One thing we all have to understand is that a running twin flame struggles in silence. They go through quiet desperation because it is more challenging to understand the twin flame connection if you keep resisting how you naturally feel. Your soul is always yearning for its divine partner.

What is the significance of a twin flame runner expressing feelings for their chaser and wanting to talk?

This a sign of recovery and healing when a twin flame wants to put things into perspective with you. Going through all the Spiritual Growth lessons leaves you feeling the need for confrontation and closure. You feel empowered to face your fears including having an open discussion about the connection that you have. It also means that there is no more inner resistance to feeling what is. A twin flame runner wanting to talk to you is such a profound shift in your 5D union because it opens up your telepathic communication channels. One thing I have learned during the separation phase is our Higher Selves keep communicating whether a twin flame is talking to you physically or not. Secondly, our higher selves are always in a harmonious Spiritual Union. Twin Flames will always be best friends spiritually.

The other important note is, that a twin flame always desires to talk to you because no one else out there gets you and understands you as much as your divine partner does.

Whenever you talk to a twin flame, you heal in the process. You feel free to express yourself because you are not judged or scorned — this is the reason why it is easy to spill your guts to your twin flame. You know they see through you so there is no need to hide how you feel. If you didn't know this, your twin flame misses you as much as you miss them because you are part of them as much as they are part of you. You live inside each other.

The Chaser becoming the runner

What is the reaction of a TF runner when the chaser starts running?

Whenever you are attempting to run from a twin flame, you have no idea how things would backfire. You say and do all you need to do to push him or her away because you are also testing the waters to see how they will react to your running. To your dismay, your divine partner reacts to the situation differently. One scenario is when they don't react according to your expectations —instead of triggering your twin flame to beg you for your love. To beg you to fix whatever is not working. To beg you to stay, your actions and behaviors of running only push them further away from you. You start feeling as if you self-sabotaged yourself. You get the opposite of what your intentions are. Then you start panicking to fix the situation. You try to convince your twin flame that you hadn't meant what you said. Nothing seems to work. You go through moments of regret. You blame yourself for making the situation dire. Let us also note that even though you go through intense phases of chasing a twin flame to fix the situation, you go through intense phases of Soul Growth Lessons and experiences. Chasing or running is healing to both twin flames inadvertently.

Dreaming of each other

I have only had three dream encounters with my twin flame during our separation phase. It feels wonderful seeing your twin flame in a dream because it is a significant shift for you. Even though a twin does not say anything to you, you experience energetic exchanges. You also feel energetic downloads. Remember that your connection is governed by your energetic sharing and communication. The beauty of encountering a twin flame in a dream is that the energetic share stays with you whenever you wake. You have better days whenever your twin flame's energy is lingering over you. You feel their essence merging with yours. You feel euphoric feelings when you are telepathically connected. Twin Flame love is blissful.

Thoughts of a Twin Flame

This is one of the toughest things to do. To learn to live with your twin flame situation without feeling the obsessive need to constantly reach out to the twin flame. Sometimes you feel an intense heart pulling that you cannot resist the urge to contact him or her. Sometimes you think stalking their social media will make the intense feeling of missing them go away but you end up obsessively checking to see if there are any new posts and updates. One misconception that I would like to debunk is that just because you have surrendered and let your twin flame have their space, it does not stop you from feeling the connection. They sporadically keep appearing in your thoughts. You dream of him or her. This makes it more challenging to surrender. Therefore thinking of a twin flame is non-stop and memories of your twin flame keep running in the background of your life. The best way to deal with this situation is to work with the flow of your twin flame process. You cannot force yourself to surrender. Be easy on yourself when you relapse because that is normal. Whenever you finally settle into inner peace, you will still have thoughts of your twin flame lingering in the background.

When a twin flame jumps into a new relationship

What do you think about this, when the chaser twin is forced to stop by the runner twin's decision to marry someone else? What should the chaser twin do?

Well, I know you have heard this already but the best thing to do is to accept the truth that you have lost the battle but not the war. Temporary defeat is a way of accepting your situation, surrendering, and focusing on healing your issues. I know it is easier said than done — surrendering does not magically happen. Your twin flame might be married to someone else but you are forced to still chase them just because you cannot stop the obsessive need. Before your twin flame blocks you, it is best to let go. Even though you are not winning right now, you have your blessings to focus on. Your life has to keep moving forward. You must keep yourself happy. Your goal is to embrace your twin flame experiences with an open. Invest your energy in rediscovering who you are. You have no control over the nature of your twin flame journey. If you are meant to have a relationship with your twin flame, his or her marriage will crumble as fast as they jumped in.

Sometimes all you have to do is hope, stay patient, and be faithful to your journey.

Daydreaming

How can I stop fixating on a twin flame?

It takes some ample time for you to learn to focus on yourself not your twin flame. You must also remember that you can stop fixating on your twin flame but it will not stop you from thinking of him or her. You will miss them. Dream of them. And you will feel the connection even though you surrender. A twin flame is always in the background of your mind. It's just like an app that keeps updating itself even though you think you close it.

I cannot emphasize enough that the sooner you focus on yourself, the better life will be for you. Save yourself from unnecessary stress and anxiety by thinking there is any aspect of your twin flame's journey you can control. Forget about trying to make a twin flame acknowledge you by doing all sorts of things to grab their attention. A twin flame already knows you exist through your Spiritual and energetic connection.

If you would love to stop fixating on your twin flame obsessively, it starts with a paradigm shift. You must accept that your twin flame is you — whatever you love in them already exists in you. "What you seek is seeking you."

After understanding that, you know your twin flame is you. You share the same energetic core frequency. You have the same energetic blueprint and you also operate as a single energetic unit. That being said, if you focus on transforming yourself, you are transforming your twin flame inadvertently. This means if you are stuck in a negative energy vibe, it affects your twin flame too.

It is best to focus on loving yourself the way you love your twin flame. Focus on surrendering to self-love. Polish yourself up. Re-organize your life the best way possible so that your twin flame will enjoy it as much as you do once a chance for a reunion unveils itself.

Runner's Fears

What is the reason behind the Twin Flame Runner's fear of getting close to their twin flame and potentially running away again?

Oh yes, the running twin flame has all sorts of fears because of some of the following reasons:

New to unconditional love and feeling unworthy of a twin flame — It is a rollercoaster for you if you meet a twin flame when you are not used to feeling unconditional love. This is the worst fear of all because apart from being overwhelmed by the intense connection, you are so scared of feeling loved unconditionally. It begins with having an abandoned lonely inner child. When you do not know how unconditional love feels until you meet a twin flame. It scares you too because you also do not know how to share unconditional love. You feel afraid of losing your twin flame because they are the best thing that ever happened to you. Instead of causing pain and frustration to him or her, you choose to love a twin flame from a distance.

Vulnerability — A twin flame disarms you in general. You feel powerless and vulnerable because you let all your guard down. You open up to your twin flame unconditionally. A twin flame walks into your life as if they already belonged there. You feel as if your twin flame can see through you. If you have issues within and deep-seated pain, you think a twin flame can see all of it. It also scares you to know that your twin flame can hurt you because they have your heart unconditionally.

Abandonment issues — This is the worst! If you were previously heart by someone you love unconditionally, meeting a twin flame reminds you of all the heartbreak and trauma you experienced. A running twin flame will run before they get hurt again. He or she assumes they will relieve the pain. To avoid being caught off-guard by any future heartbreak, a twin flame runs.

Energy Currency

Can meeting your twin flame for the first time cause emotional exhaustion?

Are you kidding me? Emotional exhaustion is an understatement when it comes to the twin flame encounter. I never used to take naps during the day but it all changed after my twin flame encounter. I would sometimes feel so tired without understanding why. When it comes to the separation phase, the changes in time difference with a twin flame also is exhausting because sometimes you stay awake and sleep at awkward hours. It is very important to stay aware of your energy and to spend it sparingly because energy is the only currency during the Twin Flame journey.

Here are some of the reasons why:

Energetic Purging and Clearing process — Indeed energy is the only currency during the twin flame journey. You constantly feel exhausted energetically and emotionally because you are constantly shedding and sharing energy with your twin flame. You feel constant mood swings; you feel irritable and easily agitated by negative energy.

You feel frustrated that you cannot find inner harmony. You also don't understand why you feel emotional chaos. You feel as if you are losing your mind and no one else can understand your issues.

Telepathic communication is also another issue with emotional exhaustion. You are constantly channeling your twin flame's energy. Your energy is also always merging and you have intense dreams. It also affects your emotional well-being because your twin flame's mood can affect yours and vice versa.

What is the outcome when a twin flame runner meets another love?

Your twin flame can run into new relationships after meeting you. It frustrates you because you keep wondering if they are happier without you. The truth is that it is tough to cope with your twin flame process if your twin flame is in a relationship with someone else. Your stress is unimaginable. You sometimes wish you never met him or her because it seems as if life is playing a trick on you. The funny thing is that your twin flame struggles to forget you whether they know it or not. Twin Flame bond cannot be severed. You can distract yourself temporarily, but a new love interest only reminds you how much you miss out on being with your twin flame partner. Once you taste that potent love connection with a twin flame, your definition of relationships and loving someone changes forever. Your twin flame's face haunts you whenever you close your eyes. You think of him or her constantly even though you distract yourself. There is a part of you that misses a twin flame. Every experience of your twin flame journey reminds you of your special sacred bond. You can avoid a twin flame but cannot replace them.

When the chaser stops chasing

What are the feelings of a runner's twin flame when the chaser becomes distant or stops chasing?

Let us admit this — the running twin flame misses the chasing whenever you surrender to what is and focus on yourself. Remember there is no runner if no one is chasing them. It is also easy for the runner to switch and become the chaser. He or she keeps wondering if you have stopped caring for them. It is a soul-shocking experience for the runner because they cannot control love for you as much as you struggle to deal with the connection. You start figuring out ways to stalk your twin flame to make sure they are not moving on from you. A runner can stalk your social media by creating alien profiles to be in the know. They will go to extra lengths to know people close to you to get updates and information about you.

Telepathy

Does telepathy stop during the "dormant periods" in the TF journey?

Telepathy is always there like an open channel between your higher selves. Telepathy cannot be faked or forced, it comes naturally to you. Of course, there is a period when it lessens especially if you distract yourself with busy schedules. You can try to not think of him or her. But telepathy creeps up on you. You find yourself talking to them in your mind. You easily tap into each other's energy that you sometimes contact them at the same time they are thinking of you. Sometimes I would respond to my twin flame in text messages after channeling their thoughts. Telepathy complicates surrendering because you cannot stop your twin flame from initiating it if they are missing you or thinking of you. Whenever you are separated from a twin flame, telepathy intensifies as a compromise for missing each other. The funny thing is that the more you try to resist telepathy communication, you feel as if you are resisting a natural part of yourself. It feels as if you are hiding from yourself. It is best to let it all flow naturally.

Running thought process

What is the thought process of a runner twin flame who wants to reach out and communicate with their chaser twin but doesn't?

The Runner Twin Flame is terrified. Any thoughts of reaching out to your twin flame overwhelm you that it is easier to stay in hiding than start another rollercoaster of back and forth with each other. The other thing is that if you are still feeling triggered by your twin flame, you have the fear that you might ruin your friendship. The running twin flame tends to have self-sabotaging behaviors. They run mainly because of all sorts of fears. It is not the chaser that hurts — the running twin flame also hurts as much. They go through chaotic frustrating emotions that drive you crazy. You cannot get over your twin flame because the more you try to forget them, the more you haunt them.

Twin Flame Chaser Fears

Fear that you are not good enough — you think that when a twin flame leaves during separation and goes quiet, you worry that he or she will forget about you. You think that the connection would fade and your divine partner will move on. This happens when you believe that a twin flame relationship can be boxed up like any other everyday romantic relationship. As you progress further on your journey, you learn that a twin flame separation is an illusion because you feel his or her essence with you all the time. You feel soul intimacy even though you are thousands of miles away from each other.

Fearing Surrender — Oh, every twin flame chaser will confess that surrendering is one of the most challenging phases of the twin flame journey. Deep down, you crave inner peace. You still love your twin flame unconditionally but you want to come from a point of inner peace and balance. Every twin flame chaser does not enjoy chasing habits. Chasing in itself is emotionally exhausting and stressful. When you have more dominant feminine energy, you feel compelled to fix your situation. Unfortunately, the more you chase, the further he or she runs from you. When you try to surrender, you fear that it will deter the nature of your connection. You also assume that once you begin to surrender, you will lose control — you will not feel the connection anymore.

Emotional and Physical Insecurities — We all have been there during our different twin flame journeys. When we do not feel good enough to be with our twin flame. Sometimes it is because you have deeper-seated issues that influence how you feel about yourself. Embracing self-love was another challenging phase because I had to break free from my old self. I shed all the negative behaviors to learn new good ones to transform and grow into my authentic self.

You sometimes chase a twin flame because you assume that he or she has the answers to your issues — this is when you think that there is a shortcut to your healing process. When you expect a quick reunion process. Unfortunately, you learn that you have to first deal with your inner insecurities however long it takes to heal. You have to surrender to self-love: You must dig deep within to confront yourself. If not, you keep chasing a twin flame fearing that he or she will find the connection with a better mate which is only an illusion.

Fear of facing the Self — When you are struggling with accepting who you are, you keep chasing a twin flame assuming that your reunion can go on before you embrace yourself — the good, the bad, and the ugly. You learn later on during your self-love journey that twin flames must be able to love each other without losing themselves in the process.

You must first ground yourself in your power and self-love to be able to share it with your twin flame and the rest of the world. A chaser twin flame feels overpowered by his or her experiences. You feel weak to find solutions to your issues. You underestimate the inner strength that you possess. Your twin flame journey teaches you how to grow an emotional muscle.

Twin flame chaser tips

What do you do when you are initiating contact with the runner?

It is always a very good idea to double-check yourself and your energy whenever you are communicating with a twin or anyone for that matter. I always ask myself a few questions before I send a message either through text messaging or email. I must say that you never feel like you have the right words to say to a twin flame. This is why it is best to always write from your heart with true intentions. Secondly, I know that it is best to respect the space between you and your twin flame so that you can focus on healing but every once in a while, it is good to check in on each other. Remember that separation is only an illusion when it comes to twin flames — you operate as a single energetic unit disregarding your physical location.

Here are some questions that I ask myself to easily assess whether I genuinely reaching out to my twin flame in good faith:

Why do I suddenly feel the urge to reach out to my twin flame?

What are my intentions for reaching out?

Do I have any expectations — Do I expect a response?

What will my reaction be to their response?

Whether we like to admit it or not, we have the innate ability to feel each others' energy as a twin flame pair. It naturally comes with the territory because you are two in one connected directly to the source.

What is running and chasing?

Running and Chasing in a nutshell: It is a physical situation that happens due to the alignment of your energy. When you go through the phase of healing, re-aligning, and harmonizing your divine feminine energy with your masculine energy. You do not have to be in a spiritual phase to go through this energy-cleansing phase. It is part and parcel of the entire twin flame process.

When you meet a twin flame, you first have no idea that he or she exists. Everything about them is intriguing, surprising, and also reaffirming that you were meant to find each other when you did. If you thought that you were previously living a happy life, the encounter teaches you another meaning of happiness. Twin Flame love inspires you to love yourself — you feel inspired to fix whatever is not working within you. Whatever brings you harmony and imbalance within has to go. You work towards feeling inner harmony and balance.

So since the encounter is surprising and the connection is earth-moving, you feel quite uneasy with yourself if you have past pain hidden within you. We all have our inner demons.

Experiences to forget, fears, unconfronted guilt, and painful emotions that we did not confront in the past. Sometimes it is easier to bury negative emotions and painful experiences within ourselves hoping to never open that box again. Meeting a twin flame and becoming awakened sheds light on all the darkest corners of your soul. Whatever you are hiding within comes out to the surface. You have to break the locks to all the negative emotions that you had previously repressed within you.

Both the runner and the chaser have their issues to deal with. The only difference is how he or she reacts to the situation. Because for you to feel happy — energetically balanced — you must heal your energies. Hence the energy cleansing process. The runner twin flame goes through his or her soul shock experience as much as the chaser. You not only have to deal with your energetic cleansing issues, but you also go through tempestuous changes. Sometimes your life feels like it is getting worse but you gain balance again as you embrace healing and the changes.

The runner twin flame, therefore, runs because of many reasons but mostly because of the need for space to figure out what is happening. You feel uncomfortable by your twin flame's presence because you are triggered to confront your demons. It is undeniable though that the runner twin flame feels the connection as strongly.

The chase seems to have it easier though yet it is not the chase. He or she knows how to embrace the chaotic turbulent situation. Maybe it is because it is easier for them to express emotions among other reasons. You usually chase a twin flame because you need some of your questions answered.

Does he or she feel the way you do?

What is happening on their end?

When will the separation be over?

Why are you hurting?

Those questions and many others go through your head. You finally learn from your mistakes to realize that all the answers you seek are buried within you. The journey that you must take is within yourself to heal and find inner harmony and peace.

The journey of balancing the Divine Masculine with Feminine energy is another interesting one.

Chaser Questions

What does the twin flame runner feel for the chaser?

If the chaser twin flame persists with the obsessive behaviors; the constant calling, stalking, messaging, etc. The runner feels repulsed and angry because the more you chase, the more it rattles him or her. He or she feels very uncomfortable mainly because twin flames are mirrors. What you are hiding from within is exposed — this is quite infuriating, to say the least. You are forced to confront your demons. Check within to figure out what is not working — why your twin flame triggers you in that way. All the chaotic feelings exist to point you to the issues. This process of inner confrontation is fundamental for the runner's healing.

The runner twin flame also feels immense love for his or her divine partner. This deep sacred connection that you feel always drives you daily to keep moving forward even though you do not talk to each other. You both have a quiet confidence that you feel the connection. More so, you are always pulled into the connection energetically and telepathically. You feel your twin flame's essence merging with yours. You constantly think of each other. You also dream of each other. You also cannot tune out the mental conversations.

If twin flames are mirroring each other, wouldn't they both be running from each other? Wouldn't a chaser dynamic be false?

According to what I understand from the lessons I learned during the running and chasing phase, chasing a twin flame in essence feels like you are running from yourself. You feel unexplained fears within that you feel too weak to confront your demons. You also know that deep down, your suffering is triggered because you have certain parts of yourself that you believe are undesirable. When you have deep core wounding and suffering, you assume that your twin flame will "fix" you. You also assume that your twin flame is the cause of your pain.

So what I believe when it comes to twin flame mirroring is that your runner twin flame shows his or her running traits physically by blocking you and doing all the runner shenanigans. Yet, on the other hand, the chaser twin flame does the same energetically. You have to first experience the running and chasing phase to fully grasp all the dynamics. Most of the lessons that you learn can only be understood by experience first. In essence, you, later on, realize that you are ebb and flow energetically with your twin flame partner. You operate as a single energetic unit. You are each other — therefore running and chasing are only labels to describe how you feel.

Surrender Vs No-contact

What do you think of the "no contact" policy related to surrendering?

Well, there are a few scenarios that the "no contact" phase unfolds — it also depends on the reason why you are going through it. It is best to leave your twin flame alone if he or she asks you to give them space. You cannot force the contact phase — when you do, this is when you seem and become obsessive. It can get as extreme as your twin flame blocking you. He or she can also put a straining order on you when becoming a serial stalker. Sometimes you get blocked on social media and from any further communication systems.

On the other hand, if you and your twin flame have a harmonious physical relationship, you can stay in contact as long as it does not hinder your growth processes. Staying in touch with a twin flame is a beautiful feeling because it takes all the doubts the question. When you have a healthy system

of communication, you easily track each other's progress.
Since you are each other's energetic support system, the twin
flame experience never feels as lonely as it gets.

Do whatever your heart calls you to do. Trust your inner
knowing as your guide or compass as you explore yourself
and your connection.

Chaser Sorrows

Does a twin chaser feel pain?

A twin flame chaser feels pain as much as the runner does. The truth is that all the pain we feel during the twin flame journey is something that is buried within us. Our twin flames are only triggers — the awakening exposes the deeply wounded parts within ourselves. When you are ghosted by the runner and left in disbelief is very a soul-schooling experience indeed. It is until the shock wears off that you begin to understand the magnitude of the situation. The initial stage of separation is the toughest because you have no idea how to handle the situation. When you are triggered to spiritually awaken, you realize that there is more to your relationship than you had initially imagined. You realize that whether a twin flame returns or not, you go through soul-healing lessons. You also realize that the twin flame journey is a battle that you have to win within yourself. In the end, it is all worth it.

The Dark Night

What are the next steps for the chaser after the night of the soul in a twin flame connection?

The night of the soul is a healing phase because you purge and cleanse your energy. By the time you are through with the night of the soul, you feel energetic purification and spiritual growth. The next phase that happened for me was a definite Healing phase which also led to immense inner bliss and harmony since I had no more demons to confront within. All the emotional pain I experienced before was replaced by inner peace.

This sacred healing phase freed me more —Even though all the emotional wounds were healed, I had scars that took some time to go away. Sometimes I would be triggered into mildly accelerated phases of the night of the soul especially if I needed more healing.

I do not know about other twin flames but for me, after the night of the soul, telepathic communication became more frequent, pure, and effortless. It felt as if all the energetic channels were opened. I could feel my twin flame's energy. Soon or later as more healing happened, the energy of oneness took over. I could not feel the distinction between my twin flame's energy and mine.

Ending the Chasing cycle

How long does the Twin Flame chaser stage last? At what point does it end, and how will you know that it has ended?

From my experience, the chasing phase ends when you finally settle into surrender. When you feel grounded in your energy you do not think triggered to chase anymore. Surrendering can get challenging at first. You assume that you are offering but are still stuck in your chasing point. Sometimes halfway through settling in surrender, it feels like a relapse. Even though you struggle with surrender, you feel a sense of inner freedom every time to embrace it. Surrender naturally frees you from all kinds of unexplained fears that you may have. You feel free to live your life without constantly needing affirmations from your twin flame. At the same time, you stop stalking him or her. You choose to focus on healing yourself. Even though you surrender, you still miss and love your twin flame. You think of him or her but not as obsessively as before.

Runner Feelings

What does the twin flame runner feel for the chaser?

If the chaser twin flame persists with the obsessive behaviors; the constant calling, stalking, messaging, etc. The runner feels repulsed and angry because the more you chase, the more it rattles him or her. He or she feels very uncomfortable mainly because twin flames are mirrors. What you are hiding from within is exposed — this is quite infuriating. You are forced to confront your demons. Check within to figure out what is not working — why your twin flame triggers you in that way. All the chaotic feelings exist to point you to the issues. This process of inner confrontation is fundamental for the runner's healing.

The runner twin flame also feels immense love for his or her divine partner. This deep sacred connection that you think always drives you daily to keep moving forward even though you do not talk to each other. You both have a quiet confidence that you feel the connection. More so, you are always pulled into the connection energetically and telepathically. You feel your twin flame's essence merging with yours. You constantly think of each other. You also dream of each other. You also cannot tune out the mental conversations.

Runner Fears

Do TF runners do things that hurt the chaser to push them away because the bond scares them?

I don't believe that twin flame runners intend to hurt their divine partner in any way. It sure seems like that but it is never the intention. There has to be one word that can explain the motions that a runner goes through. The more you try to hide your feelings, the more deeply you feel them. It is never about your twin flame partner by the way. It is always about figuring out ways to combat and control the infuriating, confusing, tempestuous feelings he or she feels. Running away is an easier option because you assume that out of sight is out of mind. You choose to find ways to ghost your partner, block the connection, and sometimes try to move on with someone new.

Every twin flame runner knows and understands the agony and fury that you experience. You sometimes cry in the shower when you are alone. The more you try to forget him or her the more you are reminded of them. Apart from that, the connection eats at you every minute of the day. You have haunted it — sometimes you are attacked by a wave of mental conversations. Even though you hide from the physical aspect of the twin flame journey, the 5D — the spiritual nature always has an upper hand.

Apart from being overtaken by your strange spiritual experiences, you change too. Your life situation shifts. You feel an ongoing compulsory transformation spiritually, psychologically, emotionally, and physically.

My twin flame runner is not running, he is chasing. He says he wants to come back into my life after 7 years of separation. is it normal?

This is perfectly normal. When a twin flame initially behaves like a runner, you wonder if firstly the cycle will ever end. At the same time, you also feel so desperate for closure that it seems as if a middle ground will never be reached. Of course, this happens mainly because you are not yet aware of the dynamics of your twin flame situation. It takes you a while to get a hang of it as time progresses. Anyway, at the end of the day, the runner makes his or her way back to you. Just like at the beginning of your initial encounter, you still get surprised when a twin flame manifests in your life. You rarely get used to how spontaneous the twin flame journey can be.

Right now, it is all about you and what you hope to gain from your reunion and or your deepest desires. You can never run away from how you feel within. Here are four fundamental questions you can ask yourself to assess the situation. Remember to always follow your heart when digesting someone else's advice. Just pick up any information that resonates with your situation and use it to make your experiences better.

ne; Have you recognized your efforts in your twin flame's return?

Well, there is something good that you are doing on your part to attract your twin flame back into your life. It could be that you are unconditionally open to embracing the changes in your life with an open heart and a positive attitude. It could be that you have learned to embrace self-love. Maybe it is the working of your newly rediscovered authentic self. Whatever it is that is bringing you positive results, keep doing more of that. Acknowledge your efforts and personal growth. Appreciate yourself for the great work done to bring more inner peace and harmony into your life. Do not stop just because your twin flame has popped back into your life — keep refining yourself.

wo; How ready are you to welcome your twin flame and maintain your life?

This is very important to note: You are the source of your twin flame experiences. It does not matter if your twin flame returns while he or she is healed. All that matters is that you are ready and healed to have him or her back in your life to create a harmonious union. Your divine partner will keep ghosting you and running away using whatever means possible if you still harbor negative energy. When you are still stuck in your past and pain and full of insecurities, all you do is irritate anyone connected to you. It is worth it and the process when you submit to rediscovering your authentic self. The one grounded in inner harmony. This is your ultimate natural state. The cycle of chasing and running ends with you — Do not be afraid to win. You possess all the power and inner strength to confront, acknowledge, and find solutions to healing yourself. There is no downside to it — only rising above your egoistic painful human condition. Set yourself a fee. You are a spiritual being going through a human condition.

Three; Do you have any goals for your future?

Sometimes we dwell so much on the physical separation phase that we forget there is a future once a reunion is initiated. Setting goals for yourself, especially during time away from each other is very important. You are both two whole beings merging your life into one if that is your desire — even though this happens, you must have your independence away from your twin flame. You must set higher goals and standards for yourself — Do not abandon self-love just because you are in a reunion. Both twin flames have to be grounded within themselves to be able to share the love without losing themselves. Use the separation phase as a blessing to hone your talents and skills. Find new hobbies that you enjoy doing on your own. Have a mind map of your future without needing your twin flame to complete the picture for you.

Four; What next? ...

The reunion with a twin flame is not the end of the journey. Rather, it is the beginning of your forever. Assuming that you both desire to create a harmonious union together. Ask yourself these uncomfortable yet important questions: Where will you live if you are to start a life together? Would you like to create a family? Do you still have karmic ties to clear before you continue with your twin flame? What kind of job will you be doing? How will you use your newfound twin flame energy to help those around you and the human collective? Remember that physical life situations keep happening because we live in the real world. You will both struggle at first to re-align your physical life situation but you later find harmony.

Being the "chaser", should I always reflect on whether my seemingly "innocent" texts are mixed with needy energy before I initiate contact with my twin flame, no matter how long I'm silent?

It is always a very good idea to double-check yourself and your energy whenever you are communicating with a twin or anyone for that matter. I always ask myself a few questions before I send a message either through text messaging or email. I must say that you never feel like you have the right words to say to a twin flame. This is why it is best to always write from your heart with true intentions.

Secondly, I know that it is best to respect the space between you and your twin flame so that you can focus on healing but every once in a while, it is good to check in on each other. Remember that separation is only an illusion when it comes to twin flames — you operate as a single energetic unit disregarding your physical location.

Here are some questions that I ask myself to easily assess whether I genuinely reaching out to my twin flame in good faith:

Why do I suddenly feel the urge to reach out to my twin flame?

What are my intentions for reaching out?

Do I have any expectations — Do I expect a response?

What will my reaction be to their response?

Whether we like to admit it or not, we have the innate ability to feel each others' energy as a twin flame pair. It naturally comes with the territory because you are two in one connected directly to the source.

Chasing twin flame advice

Advice for chasers who are kind of depressed with the separation from a twin flame connection. Yes. I have been there. It gets worse when your twin flame seems happy without you in a new relationship. This is the worst phase for the chaser. When you feel weary and depressed. You have no idea how to surrender and find inner peace — at the same time, you have no way to go back to your old self or life. I do not know about you but for me, this phase put me to my knees. I felt constantly lovesick. I cried myself to sleep. I always felt like my heart was breaking. The void of missing a twin flame feels like half of yourself is taken away. Most of the time, I felt depressed because I could also channel my twin flame's sadness and pain especially when he experienced the night of the soul.

Here are some tips for you:

Sit with the pain and then let it go — do not resist how you feel. The more you try to hide from your pain, the more you give it life. It is okay to feel the pain of missing a twin flame. It is okay to feel depressed — you cannot control it. When you sit with your pain, you are no longer afraid to confront it. Once you acknowledge your pain, you figure out ways of healing. If you have no control over it, you grow inner strength to let it pass through you.

Do not identify with your pain and fears — When we feel depressed and neglected, it is when we feel the most undesirable. All your demons come out to haunt you. You feel insecure, you feel unworthy of love. This negative thinking process is a feedback loop from hell. This is not who you are: You feel all these negative emotions because you have to cleanse them out of your system. Identify your pain, acknowledge it, and let it go.

Remember that you are a spiritual being going through a human condition — Shift your perspective from 3D to a higher Spiritual realm. When you go through the spiritual awakening phase, allow yourself to transcend. Do not stay stuck in your old patterns of behavior and thinking. Allow yourself to be renewed. When you focus on the spiritual nature of your twin flame journey, suddenly your situation begins to make sense. You trust in the divine — you no longer feel alone because you feel the connection comforting you from within.

It is a win-win situation if you stay positive consciously even though the situation does not look like it. Stay positive is a choice that you have to stick with. You cannot stay in faith only when it serves you well. You must stay positive for better or for worse. When you are in a positive energetic vibe, you easily figure out how to deal with negative emotions. You can ground yourself in a positive energetic vibe. You also figure out the different ways to inspire yourself to keep moving forward.

There is this Chinese Proverb that says; "Be not afraid of growing slowly, be afraid only of standing still." — Whatever is happening to you during your twin flame journey, make sure that you are moving forward. Do not allow yourself to stay in limbo or dogma. Changing is the only constant during the Twin Flame journey. Even if it means crawling out of your pain or crying through it, do it.

What is the best way to bring the runner closer in a TF relationship, given he/she is scared?

Firstly, you have to focus on doing things that do not trigger him or her to run further. One big mistake most twin flames make is trying to explain the twin flame phenomenon to their partner. Twin Flames have an unspoken bond — it is the most complicated thing to explain. Apart from that, it isn't easy to comprehend your twin flame journey as well. So if you have not yet figured out how your twin flame journey must flow, how will you be able to explain it to someone else? The first thing to acknowledge is that the twin flame relationship is governed by energy.

This is something that you must accept right away. If you stay in a negative energetic vibe — if you dwell on your negative experiences, it automatically affects how you relate with him or her. Negative energy is very repellent. You will not be in any position to support your twin flame. You will keep making mistakes and doing the wrong things if you come from an energetic vibe. Everything always seems to be going wrong. A positive attitude and a positive energetic vibe not only accelerate your healing but also improve your relationship generally. I have also noticed that hostility towards a twin flame only amplifies your pain. Twin Flame love heals but we sometimes get lost in having high expectations of our twin flame and being judgmental. It is easy to stay upset and frustrated by your twin flame's actions.

It is a matter of perspective though. How you view your situation is never always the right way. It is not easy to have an objective view of the situation when you are the one going through the experience. Always seek to understand your twin flame to be understood. Put yourself in their shoes to have an empathetic reaction to him or them. When you try to understand how your twin flame feels, it is easier to help him or her find easier solutions to their problems. Generally, the twin flame journey is easier when you are more understanding.

Is it common for the twin flame runners to never reveal their love verbally towards you? I feel him so intensely but never has he verbalized.

I remember when I asked my twin flame if he felt the
connection as much as I did. He was surprised that I asked
because he knew that our connection would be enough to
alert me that he felt the same way.
I said to him; "Please tell me that it is all in my head. Please say
that I am being delusional. Tell me you don't feel the same
way so that I can move on!

I felt overburdened by the intense chaotic emotions that our
connection had triggered within me.
I, later on, realized that it was my ego that needed
clarification of what my soul knew to be true — that our twin
flame connection is authentic, raw, and pure.
If you have truly looked deeply into your twin flame's eyes,
you don't have to question the connection. The Runner

Twin Flame does not need to say it either. There are no particular words to explain the feelings that accompany the twin flame connection.

The term "Romance" does not cut it and neither does the term "love".

Twin flame love scares you out of your boots: shakes you up to the core — and destabilizes everything you knew as normal just to flip you back to a life of truth, authenticity, and unconditional love.

Calm down. Everything will be alright. If you are going through a genuine twin flame connection, relax. You already arrived — you are where you are meant to be.

Chaser insecurities

What are the insecurities of the twin flame chaser?

Fear that you are not good enough — you think that when a twin flame leaves during separation and goes quiet, you worry that he or she will forget about you. You think that the connection would fade and your divine partner will move on. This happens when you believe that a twin flame relationship can be boxed up like any other everyday romantic relationship. As you progress further on your journey, you learn that a twin flame separation is an illusion because you feel his or her essence with you all the time. You feel soul intimacy even though you are thousands of miles away from each other.

Fearing Surrender — Oh, every twin flame chaser will confess that surrendering is one of the most challenging phases of the twin flame journey. Deep down, you crave inner peace. You still love your twin flame unconditionally but you want to come from a point of inner peace and balance. Every twin flame chaser does not enjoy chasing habits. Chasing in itself is emotionally exhausting and stressful. When you have more dominant feminine energy, you feel compelled to fix your situation. Unfortunately, the more you chase, the further he or she runs from you. When you try to surrender, you fear that it will deter the nature of your connection. You also assume that once you begin to surrender, you will lose control — you will not feel the connection anymore.

Emotional and Physical Insecurities — We all have been there during our different twin flame journeys. When we do not feel good enough to be with our twin flame. Sometimes it is because you have deeper-seated issues that influence how you feel about yourself. Embracing self-love was another challenging phase because I had to break free from my old self. I shed all the negative behaviors to learn new good ones to transform and grow into my authentic self. You sometimes chase a twin flame because you assume that he or she has the answers to your issues — this is when you think that there is a shortcut to your healing process. When you expect a quick reunion process. Unfortunately, you learn that you have to first deal with your inner insecurities however long it takes to heal. You have to surrender to self-love: You must dig deep within to confront yourself. If not, you keep chasing a twin flame fearing that he or she will find the connection with a better mate which is only an illusion.

F**ear of facing the Self** — When you are struggling with accepting who you are, you keep chasing a twin flame assuming that your reunion can go on before you embrace yourself — the good, the bad, and the ugly. You learn later on during your self-love journey that twin flames must be able to love each other without losing themselves in the process. You must first ground yourself in your power and self-love to be able to share it with your twin flame and the rest of the world. A chaser twin flame feels overpowered by his or her experiences. You feel weak to find solutions to your issues. You underestimate the inner strength that you possess. Your twin flame journey teaches you how to grow an emotional muscle.

Did any twin flame chasers block contact with the runner to protect themselves? Mine came back after blocking me for a year only to breadcrumb me.

The ultimate feeling during the running and chasing phase is to do your best to stop the cycle altogether. It does not matter if you are labeled as the runner or the chaser. When I was stuck in the endless separation phase, I felt stuck in a loop. I learned that it was mainly my negative energy vibration that made me feel stuck. When I was running, I felt unworthy of unconditional love and undeserving of my twin flame. When I chased, I felt as if it was my fault that the cycle would not end because I did not know how to surrender. I also felt guilty for my twin flame's behavior because I assumed that I was the cause. As uncomfortable as this may sound, you have to ground yourself in your energy. As long as you are grounded, a twin flame can run or chase all it wants, you are less affected by its chaotic energy. The moment you block him or her in case you feel uncomfortable with their behaviors, your energetic vibration automatically changes. You feel more haunted by the connection than before. You feel energetic chaos: You feel restless and helpless. Apart from feeling all those irritative negative feelings, blocking a twin flame's energy feels as if you are denying a natural part of yourself. A twin flame connection is like a stream of water. The more you try to block its course, it either overflows or detours to another course so that it can keep flowing. You cannot dry it out either can you wish it away? You must let nature take its course. I must say that when you are stuck in this running and chasing phase, you feel like the separation phase will never be over. Sometimes you try to shove your feelings aside hoping that they will dissipate so that you can move on but in vain.

Deny yourself a reunion with a twin flame or not, you will still take the same path of awakening, growth, and transformation. Then after that, you are free to choose how you would like to proceed when you feel healed and ready within. A reunion or not, a moment of confrontation comes for all of us twin flames — when you have to face your twin flame to reconcile. He or she will not run forever. Neither will you be stuck in separation forever. You cannot avoid the inevitable. When you have a chance, please stop the running cycle. Work towards a harmonious union. Even though you do not know how things will turn out, focus on your end of the connection. Seek inner peace and harmony. You are blessed to be a twin flame.

About the Author

Silvia Moon -- I am happy when I relate with you through my experiences and also inspire you to feel better about yourself and your twin flame situation to stay in love.

The Twin Flame experience has inspired me to develop incredible inner strength; I feel the impetus to achieve my wildest dreams. I have learned to align my spiritual gifts with my physical needs.

Embracing the Twin Flame's unconditional love has taught me different ways to embrace transcendental experiences like beauty, connection, exploration, flow, purpose, and gratitude.

I used to have unmet spiritual needs or desires; the Twin Flame journey has taught me the different ways of adapting to change to feel whole and enlightened. I had to dig deeper within myself to face my suffering.

I had to integrate the broken parts within: I learned to embrace self-love. The Twin Flame journey is a battle within myself; I had to stare within to penetrate my being to experience the full richness of my existence. I have transformed to reach the heights of my humanity and potential: I am creative, authentic, accepting, independent, and brave.

After I went through the invigorating Twin Flame Spiritual Awakening process and reflected on my old life, I began to understand why I felt deeply unsatisfied. I felt isolated from the world as I knew it. I also realized that no matter my social status and level of success: money, power, greatness, and some level of happiness still left me deeply unsatisfied. I yearned for a deeper connection between myself and the world around me. I previously inhibited negative patterns and behaviors that hindered my growth. I rediscovered the authentic humanistic qualities that define me: creativity, freedom, forgiveness, awareness, acceptance, independence, and bravery.

Once I found my authentic version as a Twin Flame, I gained more respect and acknowledgment of the uniqueness and sacredness of my humanity.

I hope to inspire you to feel better about yourself to find easy solutions to your twin flame situation. It makes me the happiest person in the world. While you read my books, I hope to relate with you as a twin flame and beyond. Always here to share Love and Light. Yours in love, Silvia Moon. Stay Blessed!

www.ingramcontent.com/pod-product-compliance
Lightning Source LLC
Chambersburg PA
CBHW031446130726

47989CB00003B/1293